W9-BXN-274

The World of Color

Red in My World

by Joanne Winne

Welcome Books

Children's Press
A Division of Grolier Publishing
New York / London / Hong Kong / Sydney
Danbury, Connecticut

Photo Credits: Cover and all photos by Jeffrey Foxx
Contributing Editor: Mark Beyer
Book Design: MaryJane Wojciechowski

Visit Children's Press on the Internet at:
http://publishing.grolier.com

Cataloging-in-Publication Data

Winne, Joanne
    Red in my world / by Joanne Winne.
        p. cm.—(The world of color)
    Includes bibliographical references and index.
    Summary: Simple text and photographs present a
variety of red things, including red hair, a red wagon,
and red flowers.
    ISBN 0-516-23126-X (lib. bdg.)—ISBN 0-516-23051-4 (pbk.)
    1.   Colors—Juvenile literature   2.   Red—
Juvenile literature   [1.   Red   2.   Color]
I.   Title   II.   Series
    2000
535.6—dc21

Contents

Look at me.

You can see my red hair.

Red is my **favorite** color.

5

I have a red **wagon**.

I like to pull my wagon around our yard.

My mother gives me **shiny** red apples.

My wagon is filled with red apples.

8

9

I go shopping for food with my father.

We buy red **peppers**.

We put the red peppers in a red basket.

11

I like soup.

I like tomato soup best.

I like it best because it's red.

13

My mother likes flowers.

I give my mother red flowers for her birthday.

14

15

My mother puts the flowers in a **vase**.

Some flowers are dark red and some flowers are light red.

Look at this!

There is a red bug with black spots on my finger.

It's a **ladybug**.

19

I like red a lot.

I like to wear red from head to toe.

20

21

New Words

favorite (**fay**-vuhr-it) liked the most

ladybug (**lay**-dee-**bug**) a small red bug
with black spots

peppers (**pep**-erz) fruit with a red skin
that is shaped like a bell

shiny (**shy**-nee) something that is bright

vase (**vays**) a holder used for flowers

wagon (**wag**-un) a cart with four wheels
used to carry things

To Find Out More

Books
Is It Red? Is It Yellow? Is It Blue?: An Adventure in Color
by Tana Hoban
Greenwillow Books

Little Red Book of Nursery Rhymes
by Nila Aye
Orchard Books

Web Site
Crayola
www.crayola.com
This site has a lot of pictures you can print out and color. It also has crafts, games, and online art for you to use.

Index

About the Author
Joanne Winne taught fourth grade for nine years. She currently writes and edits books for children. She lives in Hoboken, New Jersey.

Reading Consultants
Kris Flynn, Coordinator, Small School District Literacy, The San Diego County Office of Education

Shelly Forys, Certified Reading Recovery Specialist, W.J. Sahnow Elementary School, Waterloo, IL

Peggy McNamara, Professor, Bank Street College of Education, Reading and Literacy Program